French Paintings
in Russian Museums

Plate 1: Auguste Renoir, The Garden, detail.

French Paintings
in Russian Museums

RAYMOND CHARMET

English translation by Muriel DUBOIS-FERRIÈRE

NAGEL PUBLISHERS · GENEVA · PARIS · MUNICH

In no country other than France do the public collections contain such a wealth of significant French paintings as those to be found in Russia's celebrated Hermitage Museum at Leningrad and Pushkin Museum in Moscow. Since the October Revolution, both establishments have regrouped the thousands of paintings acquired by the tsars in the 18th and 19th centuries in a desire for national prestige and a love of fine arts, as well as those in the private collections, nationalized by the Soviet government. A stupendous ensemble, in quality as in quantity, worthy of the largest country in Europe, was thus constituted, which can stand comparison with the most famous museums in London, Paris or America.

Western painting is represented by a splendid collection of masterpieces dating from the 16th century to the present day, mainly from the Italian and Dutch schools, which dominated European art at the time. It is remarkable that French painting should also hold a privileged rank, especially the classical period from Poussin to Chardin, and the modern period, from Cézanne to Matisse, some of whose outstanding works are to be found in Russia.

This rather unusual situation, without parallel in the world, can be explained by the very special history of the imperial and contemporary collections. They were in fact constituted in the two periods in which French culture reached its climax, the Age of Reason or Siècle des Lumières, i.e. the 18th century, and the beginning of the 20th century, the best period of the school of Paris.

Peter the Great, who founded the new capital on the banks of the river Neva and opened up Russia to the West, travelled in Europe. He came to Paris to visit the Mint and the Gobelins factory, and was the first to collect paintings, a novelty in a country where painting was restricted to icons. His daughter Elizabeth ordered the construction of the Winter Palace, a monumental building comprising 1050 rooms, which was to become the largest museum in the world, and created the Academy of Fine Arts.

Between 1763 and 1796, the celebrated Catherine II who was a passionate art lover, acquired famous collections in Dresden, London, and above all Paris, which were to become the very core of the Hermitage. A clear-sighted, determined and energetic woman, she formed close ties with influential people in Paris. The most devoted to her was the famous philosopher Diderot, who became her untiring intermediary. He purchased for her two of Poussin's most beautiful landscapes, one featuring Polyphemus, the other depicting Hercules and Cacus. In a stroke of genius, he acquired for £460,000, half its value, the magnificent Crozat collection.

The fact that it was to be exported caused quite a stir in France. It included five Poussins, Chardins, Le Nains, the most beautiful Rembrandts, Raphaels, Rubens, and naturally paintings by Crozat's friend, Watteau. Thus the great 17th century masters and contemporary artists entered the Hermitage. Two hundred and twenty-three French paintings were listed in the museum's first catalogue in 1774.

In 1766, the Empress called to St Petersburg the sculptor Falconet, who spent twelve years working on the famous monument to Peter the Great, still standing today. Falconet acted as adviser to the Empress when her acquisitions arrived in St Petersburg. She was also assisted by Grimm, the author of *Correspondance Littéraire*, in which Diderot's *Salons* were published. Furthermore, Catherine II made her ambassadors intervene for her and nothing escaped her attention in public and private sales throughout Europe. In 1767, Galitzin acquired for her Watteau's *Mezzetin* from the Julienne collection. She purchased other paintings by Watteau from the Brühl collection, as well as one of Poussin's masterpieces, the *Descent from the Cross*. She acquired Diderot's library while he was still alive, appointed him librarian, and purchased Voltaire's entire library after his death. According to the 1785 inventory in which 2658 paintings were listed, it appears that she bought an average of 50 paintings a year. She also ordered paintings directly from Chardin, Van Loo, Vien, and kept an eye on salons and exhibitions "to keep informed", as she would say.

Encouraged by Catherine, several members of the Russian nobility came to Paris, had their portraits painted by Greuze, Rigaud and Perronneau, and bought paintings for their palaces in Moscow and St Petersburg.

Stroganov, Demidov, Yussoupov gathered the most beautiful treasures, which for the most part were sent to the Hermitage after 1917.

Three buildings, the Old Hermitage, the Little Hermitage and the New Hermitage, were added to the Winter Palace. In these and in other imperial palaces were housed the 3996 paintings listed in the catalogue drawn up after Catherine's death.

Catherine's successors continued her purchasing policy, but on a smaller scale. After Tilsit, Alexander I sent Labensky, curator of the Hermitage, to Paris, where he managed so well that Vivant-Denon, the almighty director of the Louvre, sent crates packed with paintings to Russia. In 1815, the Tsar came to Paris, had his portrait painted by Gérard and bought the collection of the ex-Empress Josephine, comprising 118 painings, of which 4 by Claude Lorrain. Nicholas I also purchased the collection of Hortense de Beauharnais and turned the Hermitage into a public museum in 1852.

In 1849, a new inventory listed 4552 paintings, classified into 4 categories, according to their interest. This abundance of paintings prompted the Tsar to sell 1219 works which were considered less interesting, although they included Chardin's *Attributes of the Arts*, recovered since.

Under Alexander II, the collections were divided into various schools. Important acquisitions continued to be made until 1914: the Galitzin Museum, the Semenov collection in 1910 (700 paintings), the Stroganov collection.

Good contemporary French paintings did not rank very high in the 19th century. Nicholas I was particularly fond of the military subjects depicted by Horace Vernet. Paintings by Delacroix, Millet, Courbet and Corot could be seen at the Academy of Fine Arts, thanks to the Kushelev-Bezborodko legacy.

However, as had been the case under Catherine II, very close ties were created between Russia and contemporary French art during the last years of the Tsarist regime, thanks to the remarkable initiative of two collectors, Sergei Stchukin and Ivan Morosov. The case appears extraordinary and calls for some explanation. These extremely wealthy merchants and art lovers conceived a passion for the modern kind of French art, which at the time was considered shocking. They came to Paris, bought a multitude of paintings, and as the Empress had done, they corresponded with the artists and commissioned important works from them. Thus Morosov ordered a decorative panel from Maurice Denis in 1909, and two large paintings from Bonnard in 1911, over 13 feet wide, representing *The Mediterranean*. But above all, he loved the Impressionists, Renoir, Manet, Monet, and even more Cézanne, of whom he collected 18 paintings. He continued his acquisitions with works by Gauguin, Signac, Marquet, Matisse.

Stchukin, an intelligent and highly cultured person, had an independent taste of extraordinary audacity. After acquiring a considerable number of masterpieces by Renoir, Gauguin, Van Gogh, he discovered the Douanier Rousseau, followed by Matisse, whom he commissioned in 1908 to paint a dining-room panel, *La Desserte* also known as *Harmony in Red*. The following year, he ordered two panels, *The Dance* and *Music*, for which he paid 25,000 francs, then a considerable amount. To his 37 Matisses, he added 12 Derains, Fauves, and Divisionists, and was quick to spot the genius of young Picasso. He bought paintings of the Blue Period and followed him in his Cubist discoveries, which discouraged even Vollard. Thus it is that today in Russia, there are 53 Picassos.

With the advent of the Revolution in 1917, the Soviets decided to nationalize all the private collections, in order to prevent the looting and shipments abroad that had deprived France of many of its treasures in 1789–1793. This resulted in a formidable flow of new paintings to the Hermitage. Its collections doubled in size, and came to comprise over 8000 paintings, 40,000 drawings and 500,000 engravings. The museums were so packed that the government decided, as had Nicholas I in 1853, to sell a number of works. Sales of sculptures, paintings, objets d'art and engravings were held in Berlin and Leipzig from 1928 to 1932. This time, however, a number of very important paintings were sold privately to great collectors such as Gulbenkian, the oil magnate, and the American senator Mellon, who bequeathed them to the National Gallery in Washington. Paintings by Rembrandt, Rubens, Van Eyck were thus dispersed, as well as a number of works by French masters of the 18th century, Watteau's *Mezzetin* in particular.

At the same time began the considerable task of recording, classifying, studying and restoring the collections, a task which is still being carried on today. A spacious building had been constructed in Moscow from 1898 to 1912, designed to become an art museum of educational interest, containing casts in particular. After the Revolution, it housed the collections of the Rumantsiev Museum and the Tretyakov Gallery of Western Art. An important part of the Hermitage paintings were transferred there between 1920 and 1930. In 1948, the collections of the former Museum of Modern Western Art, which contained extraordinary works of modern art collected by Stchukin and Morosov, were divided among the Hermitage and this Muscovite museum called Pushkin Museum, which was to become the second in the USSR. Although Moscow is the capital, the Hermitage in Leningrad still ranks first.

These two museums therefore house the essential part of the artistic treasures in Russia. Popular education is their specific object. In Moscow, 800,000 visitors, 5000 organised visits, 10 to 14 major exhibitions per year, lectures, people's universities, all contribute to an intensive public activity,

Plate 2: Nicolas Poussin, Rinaldo and Armida, detail.

Plate 3: Nicolas Poussin, Rinaldo and Armida, general view.

as does the tremendous scientific work carried out by teams of technicians and scholars.

Exhibitions in Rome, London, Venice and at the Louvre Museum in Paris, allowed the West to realize the significance of Russia's artistic treasures in the history of art. The Russian collections include items which are essential to the understanding of French painting and which have been mentioned in three comprehensive works, namely Charles Sterling's scholary book, *The Hermitage Museum, French Painting from Poussin to the Present Day* (Cercle d'Art, Paris 1957), *The Hermitage*, by Pierre Descargues (Thames and Hudson, London, 1961) and *Great Paintings from the Pushkin Museum Moscow*, with an introduction by I. Antonova (Thames and Hudson, London, 1965).

The object of this book is to select a number of French masterpieces from both museums, which form an ensemble, as demonstrated in our historical outline. The essential part of our work is devoted to modern art, in view of the quantity and the quality of modern painting to be found in these museums, from the Impressionists to Picasso—a collection without parallel in the world. As an introduction, a few earlier masterpieces will remind the reader of the presence and continuity of French painting in Russian collections.

Plate 4: François Boucher,
Hercules and Omphale,
detail.

French paintings prior to the 17th century are scarce and their merit was recognized but fairly recently. There are very few in Russia. The genius of Nicolas Poussin was the first to assert the grandeur of the French school, and the collections of French paintings acquired by Catherine the Great and her successors began with his works. In fact, there is an incomparable collection of Poussins in Russia, including about 15 original paintings in Leningrad and Moscow, several of which are first class, and punctuating the artist's long career. Mythological subjects, the sublime *Landscape with Polyphemus*; religious subjects, the tragic *Descent from the Cross;* romantic subjects, *Tancred and Erminia*, represent the summit of Poussin's art, which inspired the following ideal to Cézanne: "Refaire Poussin sur nature", re-doing Poussin according to nature.

According to Charles Sterling, curator of the Louvre, the period of the artist's youth is represented by "older, more striking paintings of a greater variety" than those in the Louvre. A fine example, *Rinaldo and Armida (Plate 3)* dates from about 1635. The subject is taken from Tasso's *Jerusalem Delivered*, a famous poem at the time, which inspired Poussin with another, similar painting, now at Dulwich Museum in England. But whereas in the latter the young woman is about to kill the sleeping warrior, in the former she leans over him tenderly; it is love at first sight, and Rinaldo is about to forget the Crusades. Armida's maids-in-waiting bring a chariot to take the lovers away. Very faithful to the text, Poussin even placed beside the river-god *(Plate 2)* a marble pillar mentioned by Tasso. It is a well ordered work, full of grace and movement, in which he shows the fresh and lively traits of his early success.

The French 17th century truly holds a privileged position in Russia, where it is represented by the most important collection of landscapes by Claude Lorrain in the world, two of the most beautiful Le Nains and paintings by Vouet, Bourdon and Gaspard Dughet, a painter who is highly valued today.

The 18th century opens with a gorgeous set of Watteaus, in particular those of the Crozat collection, procured by Diderot. There are works of high quality by all the famous painters of the period: Lancret, Nattier, Greuze, Fragonard, Hubert-Robert. A particularly charming painting by François Boucher, the painter of the graces, is *Hercules and Omphale (Plate 5)*, which was transferred from the Hermitage to the Pushkin Museum. It was made in the artist's youth, as was the previous painting by Poussin, and the artist was still somewhat under the influence of his master, Lemoine, although he showed a spontaneity which he was somewhat to lose later.

A favourite of Madame de Pompadour, the king's mistress, Boucher cultivated his voluptuous inspiration for her and by inclination. The painting's mythological theme is a pretext for a degree of frankness, and expansive buoyancy seldom surpassed. The little Cupids *(Plate 4)* hold the queen's distaff and Hercules' lion-skin, but the setting is a princely 18th century alcove, with its vast canopy and golden furniture, against a palace background with a monumental column. The painting is in the Baroque style, evolving towards its final exuberant and swirling form which historians call Rococo. Boucher knew how to use a wealth of colours, mauve for the canopy, bluish white for the sheets; there is a contrast between the woman's pink skin and her partner's, which is dark ochre. The arrangement of the linear arabesques reveals a master, whose talent David recognized, although he did not like him much: "N'est pas Boucher qui veut", or "We can't all be Boucher". This painting was copied by his famous successor Fragonard.

There can be no greater contrast in every respect between two artists than that between Boucher and Chardin. In 1766, Catherine II had ordered from him as an over-door painting the great composition *Attributes of the Arts*. So little was the painter held in esteem in the 19th century, that it was included among those for sale in 1853. Today, painters and art lovers place Chardin above all his contemporaries owing to the pure plastic quality of his work. The Soviets consider him the representative of the new bourgeoisie which was to triumph over the aristocracy in 1789, through its popular virtues of work, seriousness and simplicity. The painting reproduced here, a *Still Life* from the Pushkin Museum *(Plate 6)*, is a variant of, or rather a study for, the above mentioned composition. Surrounding a sculptured head of Mercury, no doubt by Pigalle, rolls of paper, books, drawing instruments are laid out. There is an extreme sobriety in the horizontal arrangement and the discreet tones dominated

Plate 5: François Boucher, Hercules and Omphale, general view.

Plate 6: Jean-Baptiste Chardin, Still Life.

20

by ochre, punctuated by a red book edge on the right and a black lacquered box on the left. Nothing appeals to the imagination, there is only the delight produced by the creamy colours, a richness of paint translating the tactile value of the objects, the calm silence of this vision at once composed and familiar, expressing the virtues of work and the deep peace of everyday life.

These middle-class virtues familiar to Chardin can also be detected in his smaller scenes, of which the Hermitage possesses *The Washerwoman* and a version of the celebrated *Grace before Meal*, pride of the Louvre. The Russian version is the only one that is signed.

Greuze was highly praised by Diderot, Catherine II's adviser. There are about twenty of his paintings in Russian museums: moralizing scenes, *Paralytic cared for by his Children*, portraits, gracious feminine heads. Of a more natural genre, the latter are more appreciated today. In his *Portrait of a Young Girl (Plate 7)*, Greuze attained the summit of his art. The expression is both candid and sensuous; there is an equivocal charm, and the artist reveals his talent for a remarkable luminous relief.

The end of the century is represented by over 50 paintings by Hubert-Robert, about whom Catherine once remarked that since he liked ruins, he should be happy to live under the Revolution which was full of them, and by splendid Fragonards, including the well-known *Stolen Kiss*, rendered so popular by the engraving.

Plate 7: Jean-Baptiste Greuze, Portrait of a Young Girl.

Although 19th century paintings prior to 1870 are not very numerous, they include some remarkable works: the equestrian portrait of young

Yussupov by Gros, the portrait of Count Gouriev by Ingres, a real masterpiece, two powerful Delacroix canvases the *Lion Hunt* and the *Arab Saddling his Horse*, landscapes by the school of Barbizon; ironically, there are practically no paintings by Courbet, the "communard", in communist Russia.

Corot is well represented in the Russian museums by twenty-two of his paintings. One of his finest works, *Souvenir de Pierrefonds (Plate 8)* can be seen at the Pushkin Museum. It was painted about 1850–60. The famous medieval castle, completely and indiscreetly restored by Viollet le Duc, is delicately evoked in a subtle and poetic atmosphere composition. In the foreground, two soldiers suggest the historical climate, but for the artist the essential points are the clear morning light and the wild woods; the grandiose castle is but a faraway dream apparition.

Plate 8: Camille Corot,
Souvenir de Pierrefonds.

12

colours, light blue and white clothes, pink face, are set against a red background. This example of freedom was to bear a definite influence on the Impressionists.

There are about ten characteristic works by Degas (1834–1917), the eldest of these artists, in the Russian museums, nine pastels and one oil-painting, *Dancer Posing for the Photographer (Plate 13)*. Ingres had told him, "Draw lines, plenty of lines, from memory or from life", and Degas was an enthusiastic drawer all his life, who set himself to the practically impossible task of arresting the most fleeting moment. He tried this with horse-racing scenes before attaining supreme mastery with his dancers. Concerned with absolute accuracy and truth, he intended to compete with photography and took a number of snapshots himself.

This painting from the Hermitage collection was sent to the fourth Impressionist exhibition of 1879 and is particularly significant. It represents a dancer studying her attitude before a tall looking-glass which may be guessed on the right. The flowing movement, the muscular strength of the legs, the litheness of the body, the transparence of the tulle, the clear light in the room and the view that can be seen through the large window, are achieved through a choice of essential elements quite alien to photography, yet at the same time extremely accurate. The result is a high degree of poetry and an illustration of art at its greatest.

Degas' later themes are principally nudes, pastel drawings of a fairly large size, for his eye-sight was deteriorating. One of the best but least known examples is the *Kneeling Woman* at the Pushkin Museum *(Plate 12)*. In its extreme realism, the famous writer Huysmans detected "a streak of

Plate 12: Edgar Degas, Kneeling Woman.

hatred and scorn". To this, Degas replied "I depict them (women) as animals cleansing themselves". Today we are attracted by the power of his sculptural drawings, his singular and audaciously frank compositions, the light on the naked skin, the splendid colours. Pastel drawings do not merely achieve a graceful effect with Degas, they attain the highest expression imaginable.

Stchukin and Morosov also collected the paintings of another great Impressionist, Claude Monet, who remained the most faithful to the principles of the movement throughout his long career (1840–1926). His major work in Russia is the *Déjeuner sur l'Herbe (Plate 11)*, dating from 1866 (124 × 181 cm), a sketch for an even bigger painting measuring over 20 feet in height and in width, which he subsequently reduced in size. Monet presented this outstanding work as a "manifesto" of out-door scenes, but it remained totally unknown. The continual evolution of his genius led him to paint more and more broadly treated landscapes, in which the splendid light bathes the forms in a symphony of clear, quivering colours suspended in space.

This development is beautifully illustrated by the *Cliffs of Etretat* dating from 1886 (Pushkin Museum) *(Plate 15)*. The immensity of the azure cliff, rising between the dawn coloured sky and the sea, the waves and the sails, trembling like petals, express the pantheistic view of the world, by which Monet, like Turner, was carried away towards the end of his life.

Another painting, *The Foot-Bridge*, dates from the painter's last years (Pushkin Museum) *(Plate 14)*. It represents the garden of Giverny, where overcome by a feeling of solitude, impressed with nature and light, Monet threw himself into an orgy of refined, iridescent, fabulous colours which were long regarded with contempt before being rehabilitated as the source of abstract art. In fact, the relationship is debatable. In a work like *The Foot-Bridge*, one is struck on the contrary by the harmonious construction that makes Monet a true and great classical painter.

The vast collection of Renoirs (1841–1919) covers the major part of the artist's career, from 1869 to 1902, after his realistic beginnings and before the red period of Cagnes. Most of his paintings which are universally known date from the Impressionist period, in which he reached his purest expression. Well known are his two portraits of *Jeanne Samary* (half-length and full-length), the *Woman with a Fan*, *La Grenouillère*, the *Child with a Whip*.

Two Young Ladies in Black, at the Pushkin Museum *(Plate 17)*, is a particularly interesting painting which raises a problem. As is known, the Impressionists rejected black, which studio artists used too lavishly. One day, in the forest of Fontainebleau where the young Renoir was painting, a stranger looked at his canvas and said: "It's not bad, but why is it so black?" It was Diaz. Renoir subsequently changed both his manner and his colours. However, a close look at this work will reveal that the black of the dresses is made up mainly of dark blue, with pink and light blue reflections, marking patterns in the outdoor light.

*Plate 18: Auguste Renoir,
The Garden.*

These spots of light fluttering on the forms suggest the mobility and transparency of air, and in fact constitute the great discovery of Impressionism, in which Renoir attained a natural and poetic perfection. But he wished to use all the possibilities available, and did not disdain the use of black when the occasion arose. An example of this is his *Woman's Portrait (Plate 19)* where black is used for the dark hair and eyes and serves to enhance the clear complexion and the white, petal-coloured dress.

One of the masterpieces of this Impressionist period is *The Garden*, painted in 1875 (Pushkin Museum) *(Plate 18)*. Five young persons, some seated, others standing, around a table in the garden, talk, drink, and love one another. A Watteau-type scene, showing people of humble estate in a modern world. The pink dress with blue stripes is delightful; the other woman's blue ribbon, her straw hat, everything expresses youth and happiness, in an incomparably natural manner. A play of light, a touch of colour contribute to the integration of the subjects in the scenery, in a way that achieves a refined, peaceful, unique kind of perfection.

Renoir was also one of the greatest French painters of female nudes, as illustrated by the *Nude* or *Anna* of 1876 at the Pushkin Museum *(Plate 16)*. The woman who sat for this painting was a professional model called Anna, yet she does not have the air of stiffness and boredom common in studio portraits. The artist has given her a distinction and an elegance that enhance the forms of her beautiful body. The fullness of the volumes, the smoothness of the skin, turn the model into an ideal figure of sensuousness, comparable to Titian's Venetian courtesans. The light caresses her face, but it is regular and subdued, as this is an indoor scene, underlining the body's sculptural quality. This is one of the first and finest nudes which were to illustrate Renoir's art during 40 years.

Pissarro (1830–1903) was fairly close to Monet. He did not possess the same airy quality, but was more earthy and more positive, and kept closer to his theme. The painting chosen here, *Place du Théâtre Français*, dates from 1898 (Hermitage) *(Plate 21)*. The painter was sick at the time, and had to keep to his room. He painted the urban view which he could see from his window. This was an original idea and he made the best of it. The swarming silhouettes, small as insects, the rich green leaves, the unusual, plunging perspective, give the painting a tachiste aspect, while remaining intensely true to life, an instantaneous and perpetual discovery.

The third of the Impressionist landscape-painters, Sisley, who alone lived in poverty to the end of his life (1839–1899), was the one whose paintings were least shocking and most delicately harmonious. The *Seine at Saint-Mammès* (1884), at the Hermitage *(Plate 20)*, is characteristic of the balanced simplicity of his art, the crystalline softness of his tones, the unaltered grace of the French countryside, then unspoilt. Ill-fated as Sisley was, his work radiates peace and happiness.

Plate 19: Auguste Renoir, Woman's Portrait.

Plate 20: Alfred Sisley, The Seine at Saint-Mammès.

Plate 21: Camille Pissaro, Place du Théâtre Français.

46

Gauguin's decorative colours, his exotic, hieratic style, appealed to the Russian spirit. So it was that Stchukin and Morosov collected about 30 works by this painter, nearly all South Sea Island scenes, which no doubt constitute a unique collection.

Before his departure for Tahiti, Gauguin spent a few months in the company of Van Gogh at Arles in 1888. A major composition, *The Café at Arles* (Pushkin Museum) *(Plate 25)* recalls this dramatic period. The place is the Café de la Gare; the subjects are familiar: the postman Roullin, wearing a beard, and the Zouave were both painted by Van Gogh. The woman in the foreground is Madame Ginoux, the café proprietor and model of Van Gogh's *L'Arlésienne*, to whom Gauguin would para-doxically say "Madame Ginoux, some day your portrait will be in the Louvre Museum". He was right, of course. This painting shows a clever arrangement of cloisonné surfaces in saturated tones. It is the subtle, plastic work of a painter still in search of himself.

Plate 22: Paul Gauguin, Pastorales Tahitiennes.

Gauguin's personality definitely asserted itself with the two paintings of his first stay at Tahiti, *Eh quoi! tu es jalouse?* and *Pastorales tahitiennes (Plates 22 and 24)*. The former carefully models both bodies, one against the light, the other in broad daylight; the soft, voluptuous bodies radiating a paradisiac happiness are accurately outlined, as in the Primitives. The background, in flat shades, as in Japanese prints, marks the decorative style which is dominant in the Pastorales. Everything in this work is a pattern of imaginary coloured spots, enhanced by the richly textured paints. It is said that at an exhibition, an English lady was so shocked that she pointed a horrified finger and cried "A red dog!"

During his second stay at Tahiti, Gauguin's art soared higher still. He was fully aware of this. On 7th April 1896, referring to *La Femme du Roi* (Pushkin Museum) *(Plate 23)*, he wrote to his friend Daniel de Monfreid: "I have just painted a canvas 130 × 100 cm which I think better than anything I have done so far. A queen, lying on a green carpet... I have never achieved such deep, sonorous colours before."

The painting was bought by Stchukin, under the name *Woman with Mangoes*, as it is called in books on Gauguin. But the Tahitian words which the artist inscribed on the canvas, as was his custom, TE ARII VAHINE, mean: the king's wife. Behind her head, she holds a red fan, a symbol of her rank.

The simple, primitive handsomeness of this copper-coloured body, reclining lithely in an attitude reminiscent of Manet's *Olympia*, which Gauguin had copied in his youth, the harmony of the colours, yellow for the trees on the left, blue sea, red fruit, black dog, and the deep range of greens, make this painting a true masterpiece.

Plate 23: Paul Gauguin, Woman with Mangoes.

Towards the end of his life, Gauguin returned to a more Impressionistic style, as in *The Parrots*, painted in 1902, one year before his death *(Plate 26)*. The strokes become small again, the colours are shaded off, and perspective is re-established. Yet the splendour of the composition marks the artist's persistent, hypnotic attachment to sensitive beauty.

Plate 24: Paul Gauguin,
Eh quoi! tu es jalouse.

Plate 25: Paul Gauguin,
The Café at Arles.

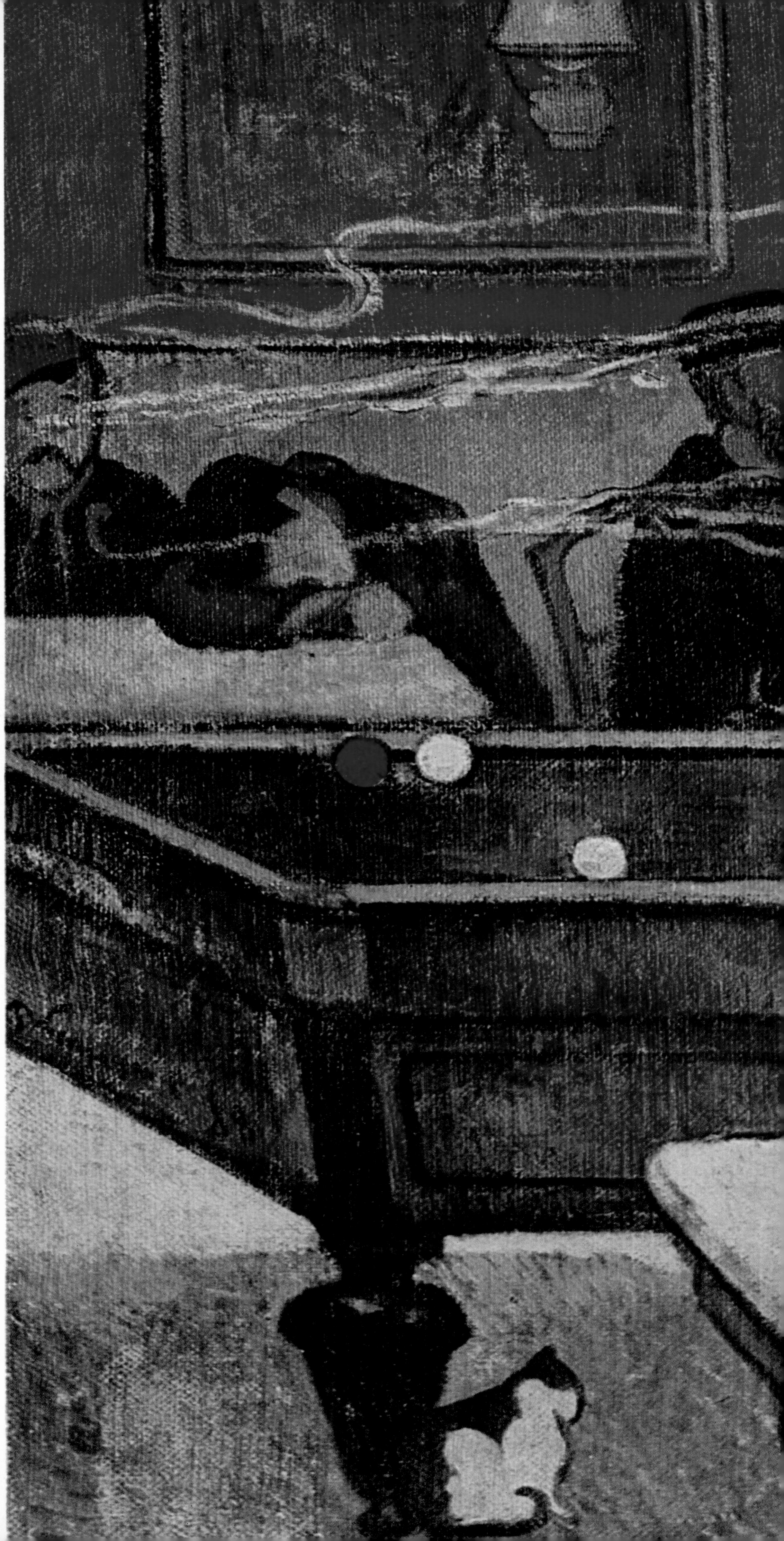

First considered as a minor Impressionist, Cézanne lived long enough to witness the start of his extraordinary success at the beginning of the 20th century. He was soon to be considered as the greatest modern painter and the essential revolutionary of art. His work came to be worshipped, and Stchukin and Morosov immediately adhered to it. Thus the Russian museums contain an amazing collection of Cézannes. Landscapes, portraits, still-life pictures, groups (a rather unusual subject for Cézanne), all his themes may be seen in both Russian museums, where the evolution of his art from 1867 to 1905 can be observed.

The *Ouverture de Tannhäuser*, also known as *Young Girl at the Piano*, and purchased by Morosov from Vollard in 1907 (Hermitage) *(Plate 27)*, is no doubt the major work of Cézanne's early period, prior to Impressionism, when he made ample use of black. His sister Marie plays the piano while his mother knits, in the drawing-room of the Jas de Bouffan house. As is known, Cézanne was enthusiastic over Wagner's music, which was hissed by the public in spite of Baudelaire's praise. The picture is a tribute to

Plate 26: Paul Gauguin, The Parrots.

Plate 27: Paul Cézanne, L'Ouverture de Tannhäuser.

Plate 28: Paul Cézanne, Mount Sainte-Victoire.

Wagner, as well as an Intimist scene paving the way for Vuillard and Bonnard. In point of fact, it surpasses them by its sculptural quality and the simplified richness of the decorative elements, which were said to foreshadow Matisse. The painting's great beauty lies in the peaceful, hieratic aspect of these familiar figures, the perfectly balanced intensity of the coloured spots, which suggests the music resounding in the artist's mind.

No other French artist painted his self-portrait as often as Cézanne; in fact he was the only model patient enough to cope with his endless sittings. The *Self-Portrait* at the Pushkin Museum *(Plate 29)* with its bald head reveals a shy, grumpy, obstinate man, attentive, and at the same time thoughtful. It also shows how very bourgeois this enthusiastic worker looked. The strokes in "modulated" tones, as Cézanne would say, appear to chisel the surface and the effect is striking. Both the expression in the portrait and his art in general reveal the implacable strength of medieval portraits.

We come to a view of *Mount Sainte-Victoire (Plate 28)*, with a tree bending in the wind in the foreground. It was painted in 1900 or thereabouts, like the numerous other works which he made during the last years of his life, of this region which fascinated him so. He told his friend Gasquet of the lyrical, almost metaphysical thrill which he perceived in the mysterious connections between the forms of the trees, the soil, the rocks, and the beautiful eternal light of Provence. With its Baroque animation and grandiose arrangement, this is one of the artist's finest paintings, and one which expresses to the highest point his mystical, visionary ecstasy.

Plate 29: Paul Cézanne, Self-Portrait.

Executed in Paris in 1888, *Le Mardi-Gras (Plate 30)* is a rather singular composition, and the most famous by Cézanne. It was exhibited at the Salon d'Automne in 1904 and its influence on contemporary artists was inestimable. From it springs a part of Picasso's and Derain's work. The subject is both fairly classical and unusual. Pierrot, Cézanne's son, plays a trick on Harlequin, his friend Louis Guillaume. The scene is neither playful nor funny, but the relief, the statuesque dimension and the massive presence of the subjects are unforgettable. The modulation of the blue wall, the tactile depth of the curtain, with its rich folds, as beautiful as Vermeer's, the tonal contrast between the bluish white Pierrot and the red and black Harlequin, have the chromatic splendour of the old masters, Veronese, for example, whom Cézanne greatly admired. No wonder it proved to be a pictorial revolution.

Plate 30: Paul Cézanne,
Le Mardi-Gras.

Van Gogh, a friend of Gauguin, tried during a few months at Arles to get along with him. Everything separated them however, their art as much as their character. The nine Van Goghs in the Russian museums reveal this Dutch painter's fundamental originality and atavistic realism.

Les Vendanges, also known as the *Red Vineyard (Plate 33)*, was painted at Arles in 1888, by Gauguin's side. It nevertheless rejects all the cloisonniste theories adopted by Gauguin. The grouped figures are painted from life and express a working tension, which the artist had already observed in Holland. Gauguin, on the other hand, loved the "beautiful, idle people" dear to Ingres. The soil is rich and deep, like a field by Brueghel; a dazzling light is radiated by an absolutely white sun, immense and fascinating. Tortured, twisted forms prevail. It has been noticed that the colours resemble those of Vermeer's *View of Delft*. This then is Provence seen with the eyes of a Northerner.

La Ronde des Prisonniers (Plate 32), one of Van Gogh's most famous paintings, was executed in 1890, at the Hôpital de Saint-Remy, where he

Plate 31: Vincent Van Gogh, Les Chaumières.

was being treated, after an engraving by Gustave Doré from a book on London. Transposed into painting, the subject expresses in a grandiose, haunting manner, the atrocity of fate, no doubt felt by the artist, himself confined. The drawing underlines man's miserable plight; the high walls from which there can be no escape, the monotonous colours, accentuate the bleak, dreary light. It is a literary work, more powerful than literature.

The two next paintings were executed at Auvers in May and June 1890, during the month that preceded Van Gogh's suicide, when he painted one canvas a day, in a state of feverish elation. *Les Chaumières (Plate 31)*, one of the first of this series, is a good illustration of the tragic turmoil which seized Van Gogh and was reflected in his work. The roof-tops are contracted, the fields seem to throb, like a heart beating too quickly. A threatening cloud looms on the horizon. An epic shudder overtakes this peaceful village of Ile de France. The other painting, known as both *Après la Pluie* and *Paysage d'Auvers* (Pushkin Museum) *(Plate 34)*, was painted during a calmer period. Seen from above, the fields stretch out to the horizon, where a long train can be seen, smoking away. On the white road, a small, solitary cart. The countryside is motionless and peaceful, as in the old Dutch landscape paintings. The interpretation of the vegetation by extremely warm touches of colour is one of Van Gogh's secrets. This work was the artist's tribute to Mother Earth before leaving this life.

Plate 32: *Vincent Van Gogh,*
La Ronde des Prisonniers.

Plate 33: *Vincent Van Gogh,*
Les Vendanges.

34

An artist like Toulouse-Lautrec can express the essence of his genius in a simple study in tempera on cardboard, as may be seen in the *Portrait of Yvette Guilbert* at the Pushkin Museum *(Plate 35)*. A friend of Lautrec's, the singer is seen here rehearsing her successful Linger Longer Loo music-hall number in 1894. She was not delighted with the result. "For heaven's sake, don't make me quite so ugly", she would say. Little did she suspect that Lautrec's work would immortalize her. The extreme intensity of her expression, both caressing and devouring, the extraordinary gesture of her black arms, the fantastic glare cast by the foot-lights, the incomparably strident drawing and colour, make Yvette Guilbert of Montmartre the most unforgettable figure of the Belle Epoque.

The art of the Count of Toulouse-Lautrec was deemed "atrocious" by the Institute, who refused the legacy of his studio to the State and found the art of the poor Douanier Rousseau totally absurd. This did not prevent Stchukin, a discerning man, from buying seven of his paintings. One of them, universally renowned, represents Guillaume Apollinaire and Marie Laurencin under the title *The Poet and His Muse. Le Pont de Sèvres,* one

Plate 34: Vincent Van Gogh, Après la Pluie.

73

Plate 35: Henri de Toulouse-Lautrec, Portrait of Yvette Guilbert.

Plate 36: Henri Rousseau, The Jungle.

of his best landscapes (Pushkin Museum) *(Plate 37)*, marks the purity of style of this 20th century Primitive. The geometric simplification of the forms arrested Picasso's interest at the time when he was inventing Cubism. But Rousseau's style, although it is well thought-out, rests on a refreshing, bedazzled vision of modern every-day life. This picture shows a bridge in the suburbs, cargo-boats, a factory chimney. In the sky, a balloon, an airship and an aeroplane can be seen, the first, extraordinary flying machines. Unhesitatingly, Rousseau would tell Picasso: "We are the two greatest painters of our day, you in the Egyptian style, I in the modern style".

The Jungle, also called *Cheval attaqué par un jaguar (Plate 36)*, dating from the last year of his life, 1910, is one of Rousseau's most amazing exotic paintings. He let it be understood that these works had been prompted by a trip to Mexico, but in point of fact he had never gone further than the Jardin des Plantes. This did not prevent him from conveying the mystery of tropical vegetation with a splendour, a primitive and lyrical intensity of vision, that those who actually visited exotic lands never achieved.

Plate 37: Henri Rousseau, Le Pont de Sèvres.

Plate 38: Maurice de Vlaminck, Boats on the Seine.

Plate 39: Maurice de Vlaminck, The River.

40

At the same time, between 1904 and 1908, emerged in France the pictorial movement known as Fauvism, whose dedication to pure colour reached a climax and greatly appealed to the Russian taste. Fauvism is widely represented in Russian museums by 7 Vlamincks, 10 Valtats, 17 Marquets, 22 Derains, as well as works by Friesz, Seyssaud, Chabaud, Puy, Manguin, not to mention their leader, Matisse.

Vlaminck is perhaps the most characteristic Fauve painter. Strong and violent, he was a mechanic and bicycle-racer in his youth, then a violinist, an anarchist writer and a self-taught painter who refused any teaching and prided himself on having never set foot in the Louvre. In art he was a great individualist. He met Derain in 1900, painted with him at Chatou and exhibited his works at the Salon d'Automne in the room which Vauxcelles called the "Cage of Wild Beasts". *Boats on the Seine (Plate 38)* dates from this period. The explosive colours, contrasted by charcoal blacks, dance furiously on the canvas. His tragic asperity marks the Northern temperament of this artist of Flemish origin. This explosion ceased fairly quickly. "I suffered because I had achieved the greatest

Plate 40: Georges Rouault, Baignade.

possible intensity and could not strike any harder." From 1908 to 1914, under Cézanne's influence, he constructed landscapes and kept to a range of greenish blues, as illustrated by *The River (Plate 39)*, another impetuous, lyrical work in which the trees seem to be carried away by a tumultuous movement, the horizon reels sideways, and the light vibrates with a murky intensity. Vlaminck's art stems from an exasperated temperament which marks his grandeur and his limit.

A very special Fauve, Rouault was also a passionate artist who distorted reality furiously. However, his underlying mysticism gives his work a deep moral and spiritual quality. Human beings play a capital role in his paintings. His *Baignade* of 1907 *(Plate 40)* is a composition expressing an état d'âme, a mood. Nature is aglow in the setting sun. The forms seem to alter and become indistinct. As though overwhelmed, the figures rise hieratically in mysterious expectation, in the midst of a timeless universe. Rouault's modernism is deeply set in an eternal Romanticism.

Nowhere, undoubtedly, is Marquet given such importance as in Russia, with 17 paintings, most of them dating from 1907 to 1911, his best period. He is a Fauve in the simplification of his forms and the frankness and purity of his colours. But his poise and his sense of values preserve him from extravagance. A clear, peaceful harmony prevails in his landscapes dominated by sky and water. In his *Port de Honfleur (Plate 42)* punctuated by a dark boat and pier, and by flags dancing in the wind, the pink dock, the transparent water convey an exquisite, fresh, morning atmosphere. A more striking example is his view of *Naples* of 1909 *(Plate 43)*, where the ineffable limpidity of the sea and the sky form a contrast with the dark boats in black and pink, reminiscent of Manet's *Lola of Valencia*.

Plate 41: Albert Marquet,
Saint-Jean-de-Luz.

Plate 42: Albert Marquet,
Port de Honfleur.

Plate 43: Albert Marquet,
Naples.

Plate 44: André Derain,
Portrait of a Young Lady
in Black.

Plate 45: André Derain,
The Road in the Mountain.

41

A great traveller, Marquet visited and painted all the ports and coastal regions of Europe, conveying the characteristic features of each. A painting of the Basque country, *Saint-Jean-de-Luz (Plate 41)*, bathes in a warm, moist light, animated by brighter tones. Always conscious of his own limits, Marquet practised a brand of Fauvism allied with the conquests of realism and Impressionism.

On the contrary, Derain was all his life a restless, enquiring artist; in his opinion great art was to be found in the museums. His Fauve period, the most striking and most sought after today, is illustrated in Russia by a number of beautiful paintings, one of which is particularly significant, *The Fishing Boats*, also known as *Le Séchage des Voiles (Plate 46)*. It was composed in 1905 at Collioure where he worked in the company of Matisse. In this painting Derain carries to an extreme the radiance of pure colours, separated by blue or orange cloisonné outlines. In our opinion, rather than the "virulent imagery" of which Vauxcelles wrote, although he was a friend of the Fauves, there is an incomparably cheerful light, a pleasure for the eye.

The Road in the Mountain (Plate 45) marks a transposition which is well thought-out and goes very far. The various elements are absolute masses, powerfully imbricated. This savage Fauvism is not far removed from German expressionism, on which it exerted a considerable influence. Yet like his friend Vlaminck who aroused his interest in Negro art, Derain returned to a more constructive style and came close to Cubism without adopting it. His *Portrait of a Young Lady in Black (Plate 44)* reveals a new concern with linear precision and plastic volumes. At the same time, he began to experiment with sculpture. The concentrated, set look on

Plate 46: André Derain, The Fishing Boats.

89

the young lady's face gives her the aspect of a statue both primitive and modern; the effect is most striking. He later turned increasingly to realism and relief with the uncompromising tenacity of purpose which gives his art its grandeur.

Plate 47: Edouard Vuillard, Interior.

The movement of the "Nabis" or prophets, which started a little before Fauvism and was pictorially less violent, aroused the interest of Morosov in particular, who acquired numerous works by Maurice Denis, Roussel, Vallotton, Vuillard and Bonnard.

Vuillard, the most refined French Intimist painter and an exquisitely subtle colourist, has only five paintings in Russia. They are all of major importance however, and date from his best period, prior to 1909. The oldest, *In the Garden*, 1893 *(Plate 48)* belongs to a series of compositions depicting public parks. Executed in tempera on cardboard, it reveals the yellow support playing between the vivid spots of light colour. The decorative trend is apparent but it is subordinated to a supple composition in which the eye discovers the scenery with enchantment. The light touches, giving the illusion of light and shade, quiver like petals. The *Interior* of 1904 *(Plate 47)* bears witness to Vuillard's perfection as a painter of Parisian indoor scenes of the early 20th century. It is a sheltered, silent and peaceful world, where the subjects are surrounded by an abundance of furniture, objects, mirrors and especially carpets, drapings, material,

*Plate 48: Edouard Vuillard,
In the Garden.*

93

all described by Vuillard with infinite sensitiveness. The profusion of shimmering light and colour is as acute as the literary analyses of Marcel Proust. A step is made towards simplicity in *Children Playing at the Window*, 1909 *(Plate 49)*. The plunging perspective leaves a big empty space in the foreground, balanced by a dark carpet. The milky white light pouring in through the open window fills the entire canvas. The silhouettes of the two children are very natural and convey the acute vibration and deep charm of life. Such art is in the tradition of Vermeer and Chardin.

Bonnard, the greatest of the Nabis, is widely represented in the Russian collections with 13 paintings dating from 1895 to 1912. Two large canvases 123 cm wide form a pair, *Morning in Paris* and *Evening in Paris* (Hermitage) *(Plate 53)*. This is a street scene, taken from close up, contrary to the Impressionist manner. The subjects over-flow from the frame to the right and to the left. Strollers, hawkers, a dog, a donkey-cart, housewives, the people of Paris are observed with spirit and kindliness. The colours are delicate and hazy in the pink evening light. Even the houses seem to fade and soften. It is realism seen with a smile of happiness.

Like his friend Vuillard, Bonnard also painted indoor scenes. One of the most interesting is the *Cabinet de Toilette* (Pushkin Museum) *(Plate 52)*. It is a surprising composition: a rather modest dressing-table stands against a window. On top of it is a mirror in which are reflected a chest of drawers, a child eating his breakfast, and an opulent nude seen from the back. The harmony in white and blue, punctuated by yellow spots, is delicate and clear, and the nude's pink flesh, cut by the mirror, achieves a sensuous quality. The painter's temperament, freer than Vuillard's, reveals itself further still in his marvellous landscapes: *Premier Printemps* or *Les Petits*

Plate 49: Edouard Vuillard, Children playing at the Window.

Plate 50: Pierre Bonnard, The River.

Plate 51: Pierre Bonnard, Premier Printemps.

Plate 52: Pierre Bonnard, Cabinet de Toilette.

Plate 53: Pierre Bonnard, Evening in Paris.

Plate 54: Kees Van Dongen, Dancer in Red.

Plate 55: Kees Van Dongen, Lady with a Black Hat.

Faunes (Plate 51), and *The River (Plate 50)*. The clear perspective is marked by the refined modulation of colours, the quivering beauty of the light. Tones overlap and succeed one another in ever renewed patterns. A rich, decorative harmony suggests the intense, fresh and dazzling presence of the outside world. It shows a close and rarely achieved combination of reality and sensitive poetry.

Two paintings by Van Dongen are typical of the generous, truculent style adopted by this Dutch master of the school of Paris. The *Lady with a Black Hat (Plate 55)*, a proud and seducing beauty, with her huge hat, the rich drapery of her green costume, raises fashion to the highest level. A bright yellow spot on her face, and another in Veronese green, are a tasteful illustration of Fauvist audacity. The other painting, *Dancer in Red (Plate 54)* is of a freer style. Practically overflowing from the frame, she suggests a powerful, fleshly presence, overwhelming sensuality, and at the same time a harmonious beauty and a great joie de vivre.

Since the Revolution, a number of modern paintings were donated to the Russian museums by their authors, Rivera, Guttuso and the French painters Matisse and Fernand Léger. *The Post-Card (Plate 56)* is a major composition by the latter. The style is mature; it is a decorative and monumental assembly of disparate elements: two naked bodies, plants, a stamp, abstract forms, heavily outlined and set in relief. An original synthesis of Cubism and Realism, Léger's art asserts itself by its distinct, frank and decisive impact.

Plate 56: Fernand Léger,
The Post-Card.

Matisse and Picasso dominate the Russian collections of modern French paintings, with over 50 canvases each. These unique collections were acquired thanks to Stchukin's intuition, who recognized those who today are unanimously considered as the century's greatest masters, at a time when their talent was widely questioned.

Stchukin acquired his first Matisses in 1904, when he visited the Paris exhibitions. He met the artist in 1906 and thereafter bought paintings of increasing importance directly from him, and ordered the huge decorative panels known as *The Dance* and *Music* for his palace. In 1911, he invited Matisse to Moscow. He assembled 37 works by Matisse and induced his friend Morosov to buy a dozen. Until 1914, Stchukin was Matisse's chief patron and source of income.

Matisse was born in 1869. At the Beaux-Arts, he was a pupil of Gustave Moreau, who predicted: "You will simplify painting". His art evolved gradually. One of his earliest works to be found in Russia, *Still Life*, also called *Vaisselle et Fruits*, painted in 1901 *(Plate 59)*, reveals that after

Chardin, he came under the influence of Cézanne, whom he greatly admired. In fact, although he was in need of money, he bought a little painting by Cézanne, *Bathers*, which he kept always. The plastic quality of this work is marked, and the modulation of the bright colours reveals the greatest care.

He was subsequently attracted by Divisionist and Fauvist experiments. During a trip to Collioure in 1906, he simplified his style, reduced his volumes, which he bathed in a beautiful light, and devoted himself to the joy of pure colour. A strange painting, *Lady on a Terrace, Venice*, dating approximately from 1907 *(Plate 60)*, may have been executed during a trip to Italy. The strongly outlined flat shades are Fauvist, with a marked influence of Japanese prints. The light arrangement of the juxtaposed colours and the absence of shadows suggest an equal and intense reverberation of the summer light. The very beautiful *Nude* of 1905, known as *Noir et Or (Plate 63)*, reveals another aspect of Fauvism. Its powerful, almost brutal, relief is reminiscent of the sculpture produced by Matisse at that period. The simple tonality is extremely luminous and the vigorous forms had a marked influence on German Expressionists.

The evolution towards a bare, concise style was quickened in the following years. In 1908, he painted a big composition which he called *Harmony in Green*. He took it up again and turned it into a *Harmony in Blue*, sold it to Stchukin as a "decorative panel for a dining-room", and exhibited it at the Salon d'Automne. Yet he kept it a while longer, and changed it into a *Harmony in Red*. However, the acquirer does not seem to have minded this when he received the composition in 1909. It is a truly admirable work. On a red background, light blue patterns are designed, punctuated by bright yellow fruit. On the right, a blonde figure wearing a black bodice answers someone at the window on the left; in the middle, a fresh, stylized landscape.

The bareness of his art is accentuated in two compositions with figures, *The Game of Bowls*, 1908 *(Plate 61)*, and *Nymph and Satyr*, 1909 *(Plate 62)*. The former shows ochre figures, on a very plain light green background, under a strip of blue sky. The dark, round heads are like counterparts for the dark bowls. The supple curves of the bodies constitute a harmonious correspondence between forms, which marks the triumph of pure painting. The accurate representation of reality is not abandoned however, in this case the movements of human beings at play and in the midst of desire.

In 1911, on his return from a trip to Spain, Matisse painted two large indoor scenes which Stchukin bought from him, *The Artist's Family*, and *The Artist's Studio* (181 × 221 cm), Pushkin Museum *(Plate 58)*. It is typical of the return to reality which Matisse effected mainly after 1918. The drawing remained simplified, there were no shades, almost no reliefs, but the depth is indicated by the lines in the carpet. The items shown in this work mark the artist's various activities: six paintings, two sculptures, one drawing. His particular liking for material with decorative designs no doubt increased following his discovery of Spain. The essential quality remains the chromatic harmony, particularly subtle and refined. The range of yellow and greens is extremely delicate. Both are contained in the splendid draping hanging in the middle of the room.

Les Poissons rouges (Plate 57) also dates from 1911. It is a famous painting, and perhaps the most attractive. Big leaves, flowers, the arm of

Plate 57: *Henri Matisse, Les Poissons rouges.*

Plate 58: *Henri Matisse, The Artist's Studio.*

Plate 59: *Henri Matisse, Still Life.*

Plate 60: *Henri Matisse, Lady on a Terrace, Venice.*

Plate 61: *Henri Matisse, The Game of Bowls.*

Plate 62: *Henri Matisse, Nymph and Satyr.*

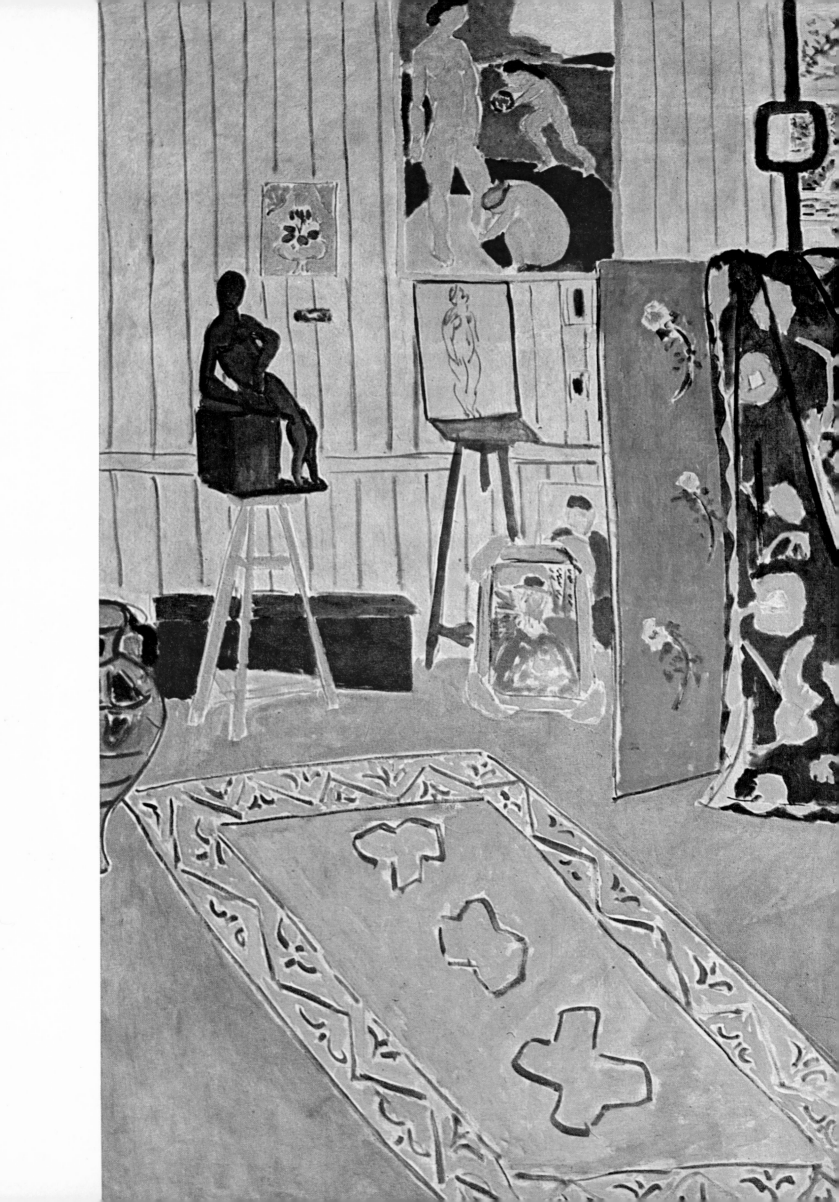

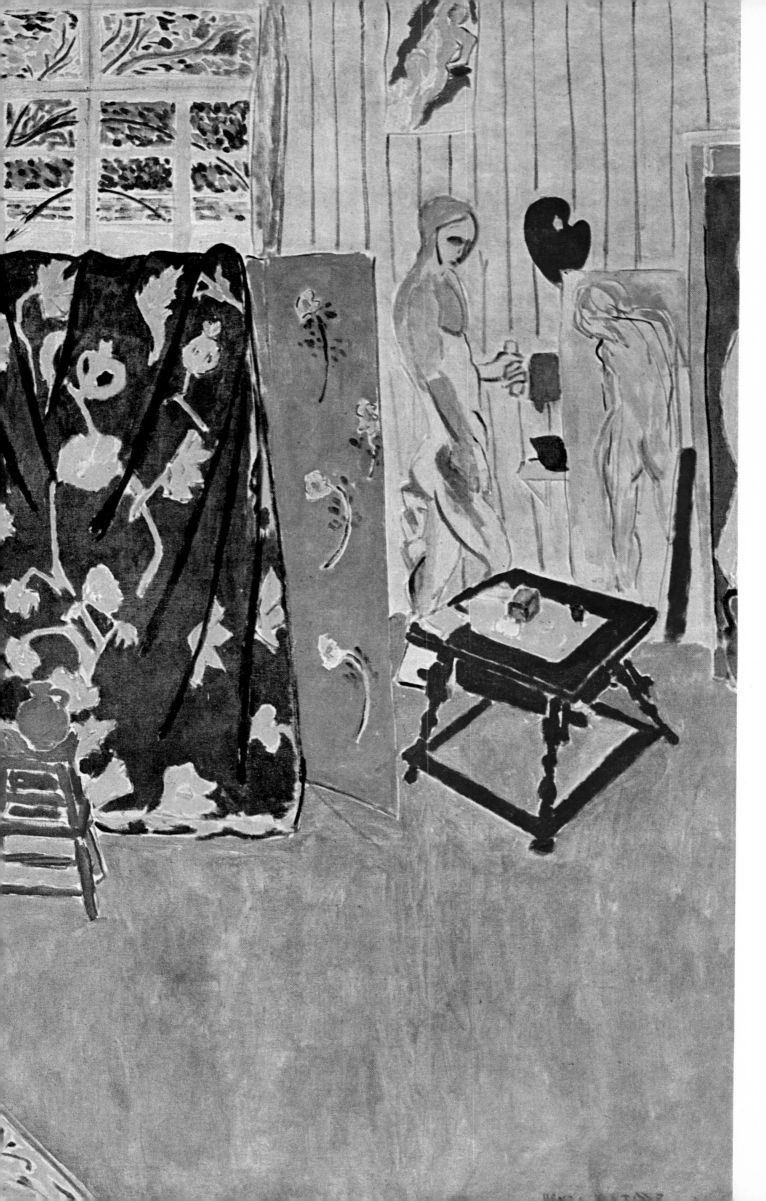

a chair, a pink table on a black background, are haphazardly but decoratively arranged around a large, transparent vase, in which four fish swim. They can be seen on the surface by refraction. Here and there, the white canvas can be spotted through the light paint. The marvellous gold-fish seem to glide irresistibly and arrest the eye. The extraordinary thing in this painting is the hallucinating realism of the trompe-l'œil effect created with such simple means by a painter who interpreted nature with the greatest depth of feeling.

The collection of Matisses includes many other outstanding works, including the *Portrait of Madame Matisse*, the *Moroccan in Green*, *Les Capucines* and the panel *The Dance*, without which one cannot possibly have an accurate idea of his work prior to 1914. *Portrait of a Woman*, 1947 *(Plate 64)*, shows his ultimate evolution towards a simplification of forms in flat tints of plain colours, circled like stained glass elements, in a nearly geometrical clearness, which was to lead to his famous papiers découpés.

Plate 63: Henri Matisse,
  Nude.

It was Matisse who led Stchukin, one day in 1908, to Picasso's studio, an artist twelve years younger than himself. It was a generous move, uncommon among painters. Fernande Olivier, Picasso's companion, told of the impression this unusual visitor made on her: "He was small and pale, with a rather pig-like face, and he stammered terribly". The drawing which Matisse made of him is less severe. Stchukin immediately bought two canvases, at a very high price. He was to acquire fifty paintings until 1914, and his friend Morosov three. He was enthusiastic over all the painter's successive manners. There was a difficult moment when Picasso showed *Les Demoiselles d'Avignon*; Gertrude Stein recalls that Stchukin, in tears, told her "What a loss for French art!". He nevertheless continued to buy Picassos, from the artist and from Kahnweiler, whose cables and messages he never failed to answer.

The Blue Period, 1901–1904, which was long Picasso's most appreciated, is particularly well represented in the Russian museums. The *Portrait of Jaime Sabartès*, known as *Le Bock*, 1901 *(Plate 69)*, is the portrait of a young poet who remained until his death the closest and most faithful of Picasso's friends, his secretary, historiographer, and occasionally his

Plate 64: Henri Matisse, Portrait of a Woman.

Plate 65: Pablo Picasso, Portrait of Soler.

Plate 66: Pablo Picasso, La Rencontre.

116

scapegoat. Extremely short-sighted, he always wore glasses and had a mustache, both of which Picasso did away with, giving him a melancholic, romantic quality typical of his works of that period. Picasso mastered drawing in his childhood, and the summary shortening of the right arm shows that he had already stopped caring about strict accuracy. The elongated shapes, tapered hands, the already apparent geometric tendency, underline the strikingly intense expression of solitude and sadness. The *Portrait of Soler*, 1903 *(Plate 65)*, represents a tailor of Barcelona and friend of Picasso. When the artist was completely destitute, he paid for his suits with paintings. Once he even burnt his now priceless aquarelles to heat his studio. This particular work was still in the Blue Period style; the drawing is very classical, no doubt to satisfy the model, and there is an air of gravity and dignity which is very Spanish. The quality of the beautiful white spot of the collar undoubtedly reveals the influence of Cézanne, whose works he had seen at Vollard's, where he held his first Paris exhibition. *La Rencontre*, 1903 *(Plate 66,* reproducing the upper section of the painting), a canvas 152 × 100 cm, is one of the major compositions of this period. An unmistakable air of Spanish misery pervades the work, a memory of the people of Barcelona perhaps. However, the theme's general significance goes beyond reality. The Visitation is evoked, a recurrent theme in Christian art. Its interpretation here is both profane and human. Two unhappy women gently confide in one another. The effect is of a singularly moving grandeur. It is amazing that such a young artist —he was only twenty-two at the time—could convey as much feeling and experience.

The Blue Period was followed by the Rose Period, whose colour and inspiration correspond to an easier moment for Picasso, who was in less

Plate 67: Pablo Picasso, Nude.

straitened circumstances. One of the major compositions of this period is the big canvas of *The Acrobat with a Ball*, 1905 (164 × 94 cm) *(Plate 70)*. Acrobats and tumblers were themes which fascinated Picasso at the time. His colours became light and clear, his forms graceful, the atmosphere luminous. His subject no longer seemed as oppressed by life. A certain joy can be sensed in the frail girl poised on the ball. In contrast, the back view of the seated athlete, muscular as an antique statue, describes a colossal power. The Mediterranean spirit, underlying all Picasso's work, triumphally reappears in this painting. There was always the risk that it might turn into academism, even with Picasso, but in this particular instance it was invigorated by the artist's sensitiveness which reached a point of exacerbation in the Blue Period.

A trace of melancholy subsists in the beautiful *Woman of Majorca (Plate 68)*, one of the artist's most attractive and harmonious works, painted before he took to producing monstrous apparitions. It is a tribute to Mediterranean grace and elegance. This woman from Majorca, an island conquered by the Greeks and the Romans, bears the refinement of a Tanagra statue, combined with Spanish dignity and Hellenic distinction. The sober assurance in the tempera and water-colour on an ochre cardboard which can be detected here and there, as in Vuillard's works, the linear purity, particularly in the hand, denote the drawing of a master. Picasso could easily have fallen into academism, prevailing among the fashionable painters of the period who painted subjects of a worldly elegance.

When he felt this danger approaching, he turned to the Iberian Primitives and to Negro Art. He composed *Les Demoiselles d'Avignon* before entering

Plate 68: Pablo Picasso, Woman of Majorca.

into Cubism. Although Stchukin shrank back before the aggressiveness of this famous composition, he acquired other works which were fairly close to it, *Three Women* and *The Dryad*. Illustrated here is a *Nude* of 1907 *(Plate 67)*, a monochrome painting in which the facial planes appear chiselled like a Negro mask. The artist's experiment with volumes is in fact a reaction against literary and sentimental traps, and against affectation, a danger which had previously threatened him. He wished to produce a work of pure painting, to reconquer the sculptural strength of matter and no doubt also to experiment and startle the public, without fear of shocking them. This led him rapidly to Cubism. Stchukin unhesitatingly followed him in his new venture which disconcerted almost all his friends, and continued to buy major works from him, *Violin and Glass* and the celebrated *Portrait of Ambroise Vollard* in particular. He constituted the most complete collection of Picasso's works prior to 1914.

Plate 69: Pablo Picasso,
Portrait of Jaime Sabartès.

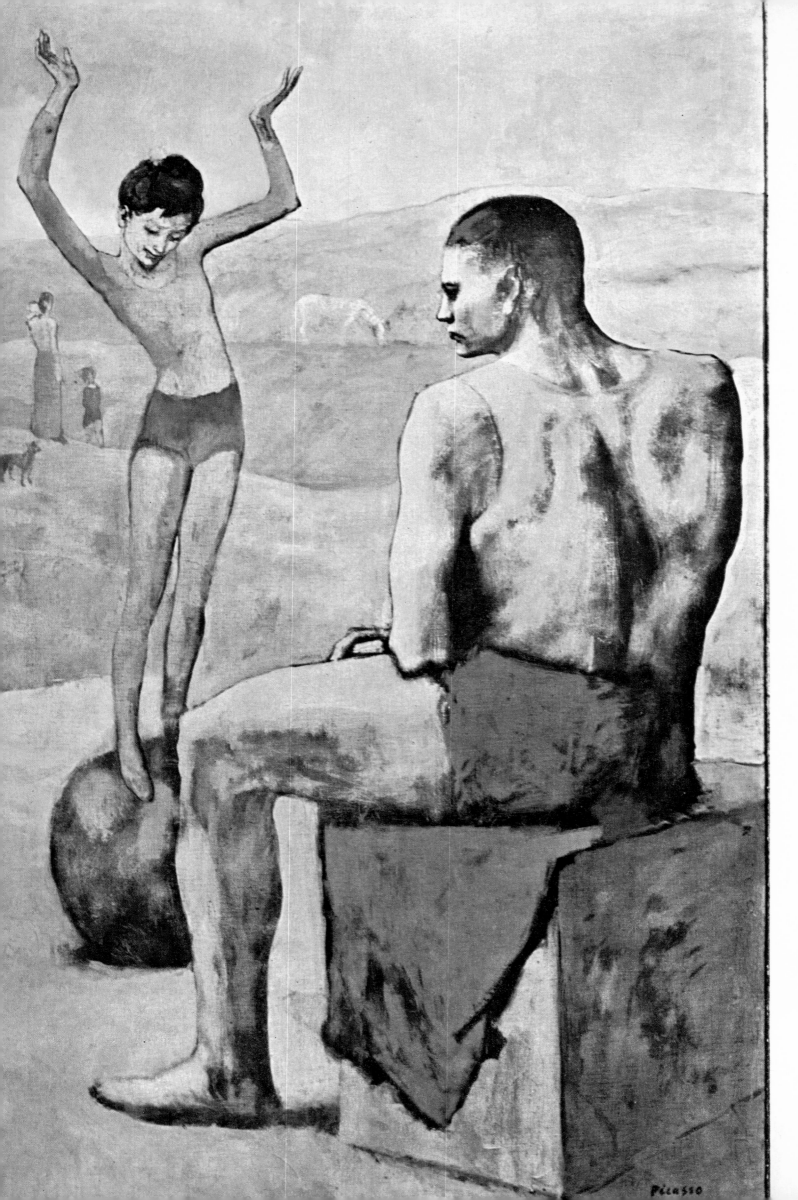

Picasso

There are about 1200 French paintings at the Hermitage in Leningrad and the Pushkin Museum in Moscow. Quantity in art is not as negligible a matter as is sometimes claimed. Thanks to their clear-sightedness and intuition, Catherine II, Stchukin and Morosov acquired a considerable number of works in order to include the major paintings in their collections. They constitute a most striking panorama of French painting at its noblest and most moving.

Plate 70: Pablo Picasso,
The Acrobat with a Ball.

GENERAL TABLE OF ILLUSTRATIONS

Photographs:
—Editions Cercle d'Art, Paris: Plates 8, 10 to 12, 23, 35 to 37, 39 to 52 and 68.
—All the other photographs were taken by Gérard Bertin for Les Editions Nagel, Geneva.

INDEX

133

Printed in Switzerland

PRINTED IN MAY 1970
ON THE PRESSES OF NAGEL PUBLISHERS, GENEVA

THE BINDING WAS EXECUTED IN THE WORKSHOPS OF
NAGEL PUBLISHERS, GENEVA

TYPOGRAPHIC PLATES ENGRAVED BY CLICHÉS UNION, PARIS
AND OFFSET COLOR SEPARATION BY PHOTOLITHOS AGRAF, GENEVA
AND PHOTO-CHROMO-GRAVURE, LYONS

THE PUBLISHER'S LEGAL DEPOSIT IS 511

PRINTED IN SWITZERLAND